2

Recorder Duets
from the Beginning

John Pitts

Duet playing brings extra pleasure to all involved, and with it an incentive to learn new notes and rhythms in order to succeed. A simultaneous development of listening skills and concentration is also required for successful ensemble playing.

Recorder Duets from the Beginning Books 1, 2 and *3* provide a wide range of repertoire to encourage duet playing by descant recorder players, both accompanied and unaccompanied. All the items are carefully graded, both in range of notes (pitches) included and in the level of difficulty. It is expected that players using Book 2 will have already reached the end of *Recorder from the Beginning Book 2*, in the author's widely popular teaching scheme.

Early pieces have matching rhythms in both parts, making it easier for the players to keep in time together. Then some independence of parts is gradually introduced, including the use of imitation and counting of rests, plus more sophisticated rhythms.

The Pupil's Books include guitar chord symbols, and the Latin American items have suggestions for use of percussion instruments. The Teacher's Books include piano accompaniments for all the duets as well as the Latin American percussion parts.

In keeping with the 'repertoire' nature of the books, only a minimum of teaching help or explanation is given. Where more help is required it is best to refer to the appropriate pages of the teaching scheme *Recorder from the Beginning*.

Chester Music Limited

Contents

*Notes listed as 'included' do not necessarily appear often in the piece.
Some may occur only once or twice in a piece!
It is best to assess each item individually.

Spring (from The Four Seasons) Vivaldi

The Italian **Antonio Vivaldi** (1678-1741) wrote many violin concertos, several with descriptive titles as used here.

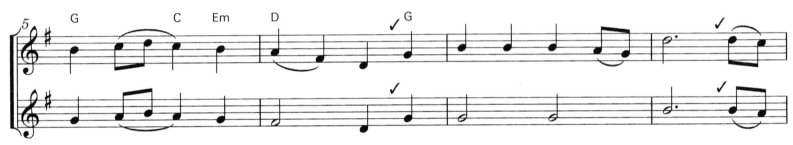

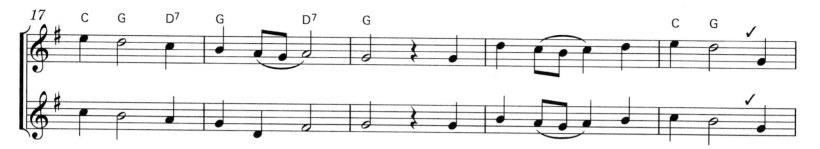

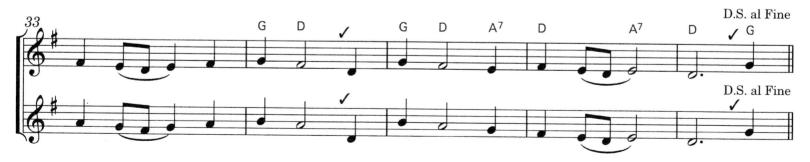

Ade, zur guten Nacht   German

Introduction: count 4 bars (see Teacher's Book)

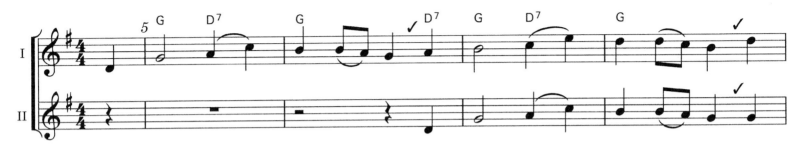

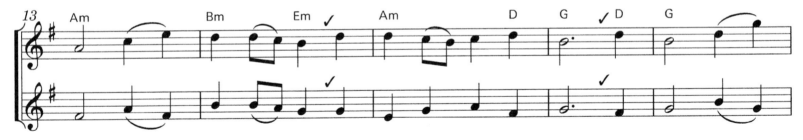

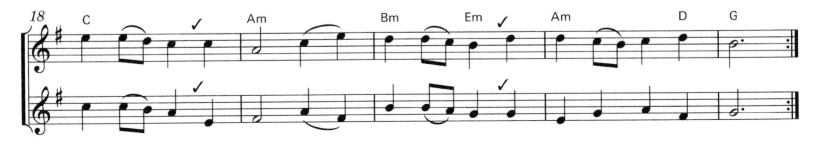

Gay Gordons   Scottish

Introduction: count 4 bars (see Teacher's Book)

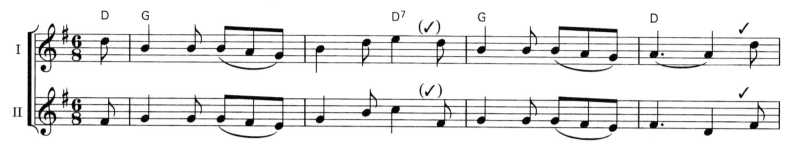

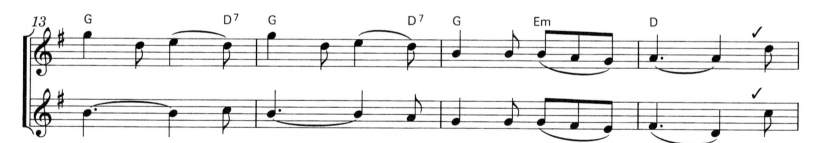

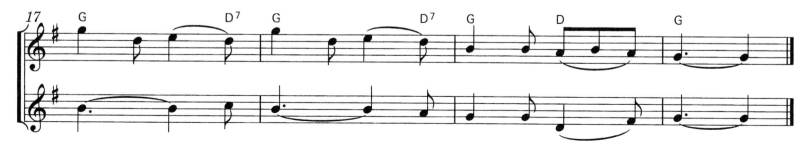

Drink To Me Only   English

Introduction: count 4 bars

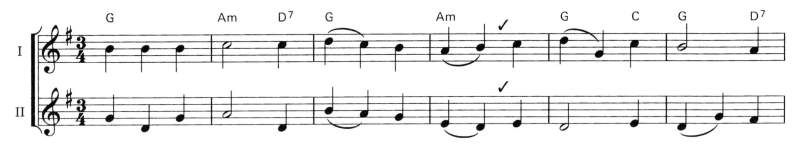

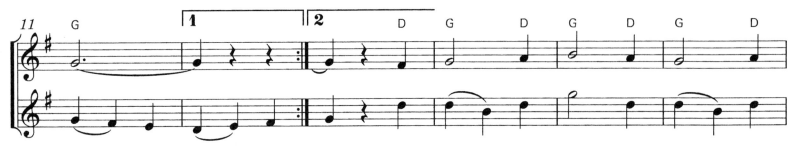

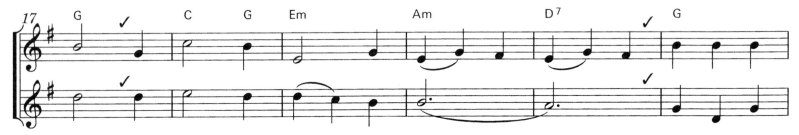

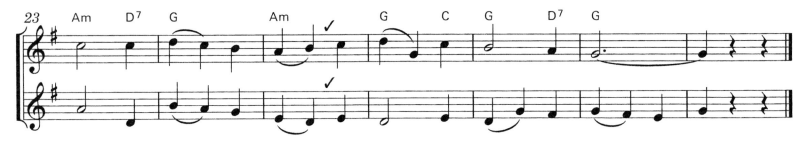

Star of County Down   Irish

Introduction: count 2 bars (see Teacher's Book)

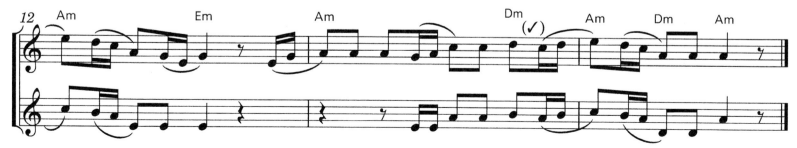

Waltz   Schubert

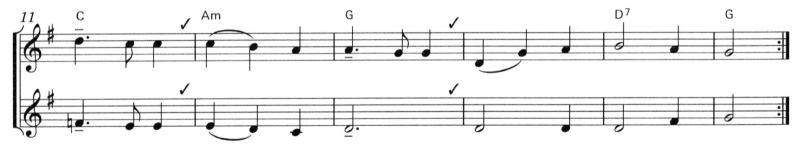

Franz **Schubert** (1797 - 1828) was a German composer. He wrote over 600 songs as well as symphonies, string quartets and piano music. The **waltz** was a German ballroom dance that first became very popular about 1800. It has a strong rhythm of three beats in a bar. As you play, try to accent the marked notes to help the music to swing along like a dance.

Cossack Dance   Pitts

Introduction: count 2 bars

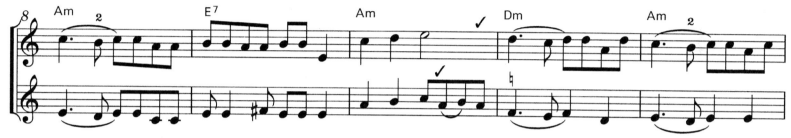

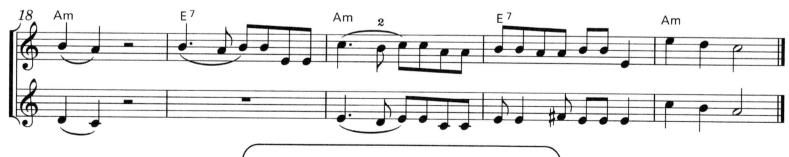

2 = optional alternative fingering. See page 32.

Santa Lucia   Neopolitan

Introduction: count 2 bars

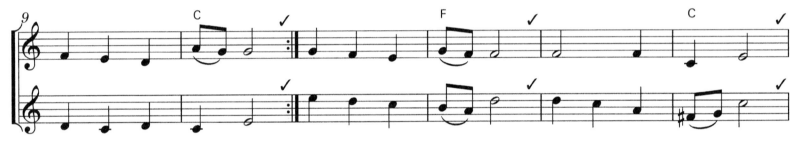

Crombie's Boogie   Pitts

Introduction: count 2 bars

With a steady swing (♩ = 106)

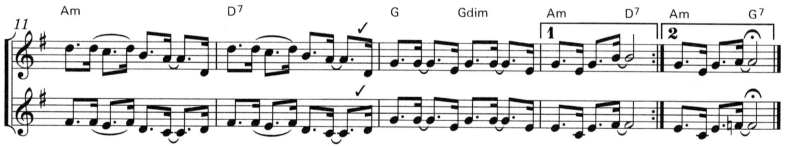

Playing the tied notes

First play this:
Take care with the slur and
accent the G marked >

Now join (tie) both
G notes together:

Pretty Peña Mexican

Introduction: count 4 bars

Portuguese Dance

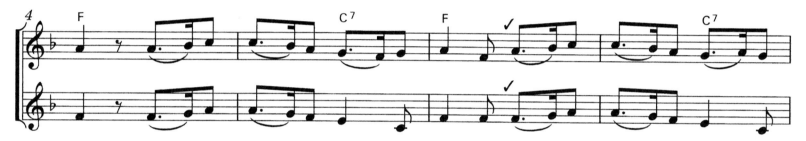

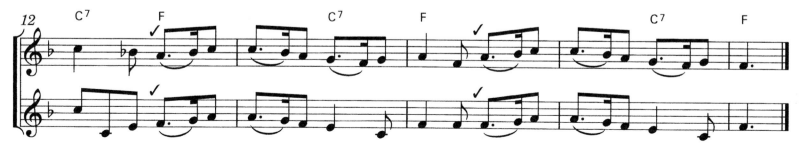

Cielito Lindo   Mexican

Introduction: count 4 bars

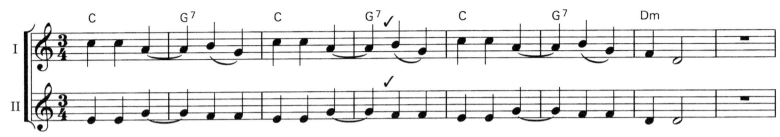

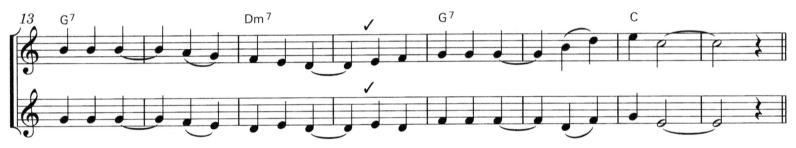

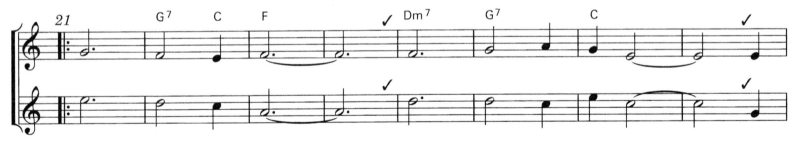

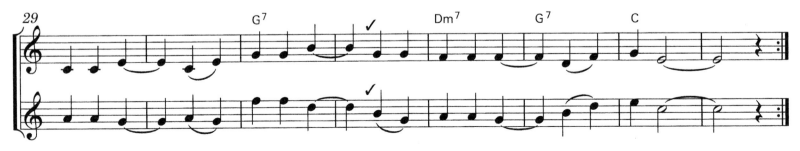

Plaisir d'amour   Martini

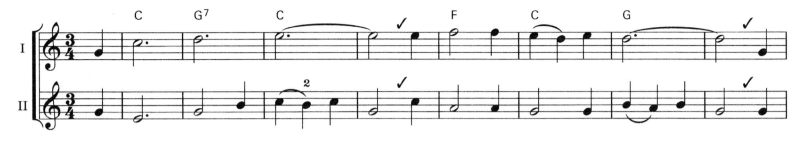

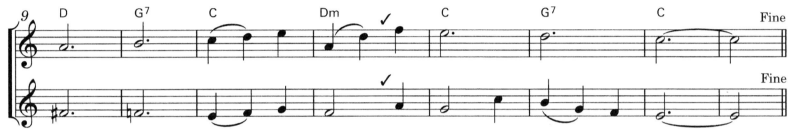

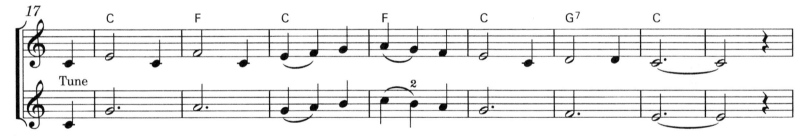

2 = optional alternative fingering.

The Saints

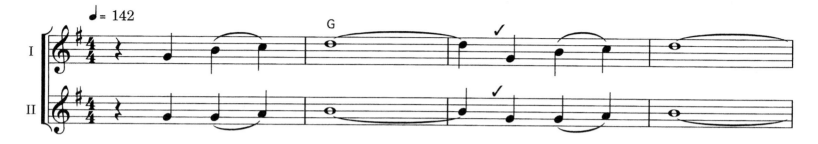

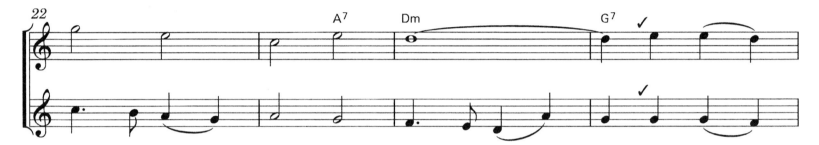

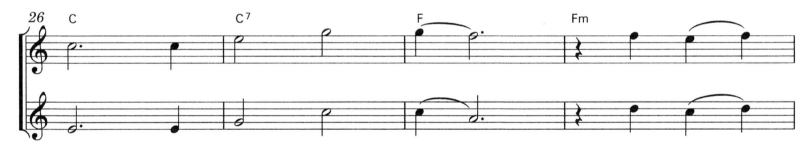

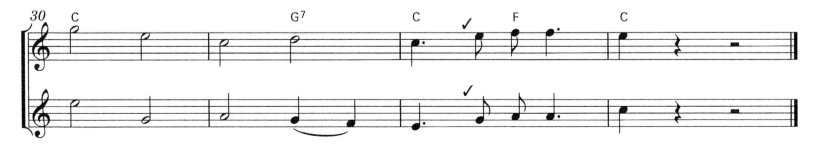

O Waly Waly   English

Czech Polka J. Strauss

Introduction: count 4 bars (see Teacher's Book)

The **polka** is a lively dance from Czechoslovakia. It became popular throughout Europe in the 19th century.

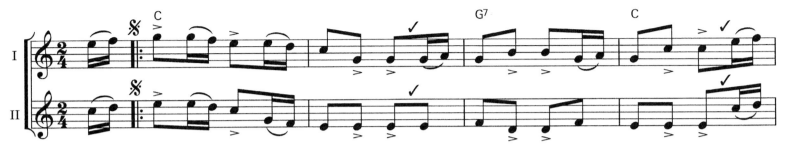

Ragtime   Pitts

Introduction: count 4 bars

Ragtime was a type of early American jazz music. The melody is strongly syncopated against a steady accompaniment.

Not too fast

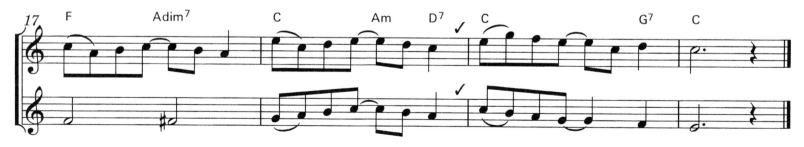

22

Churchill's March

This music is from **The English Dancing Master**, published in London by John Playford in 1651.

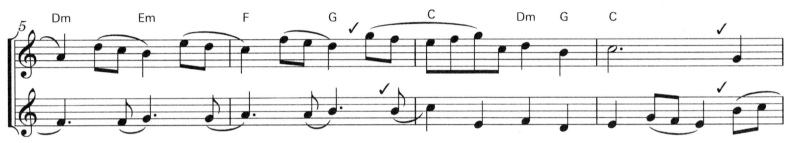

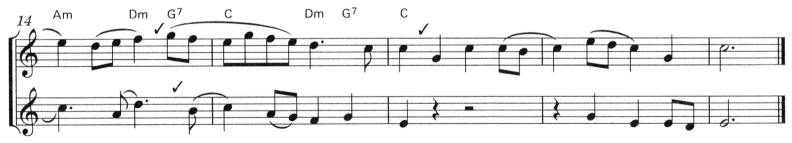

Polka for Paula   Pitts

Introduction: count 4 bars

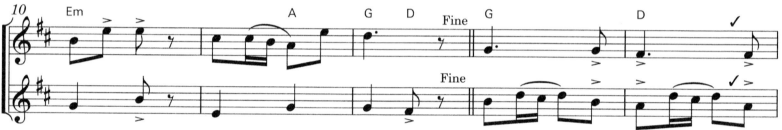

March from Scipio   Handel

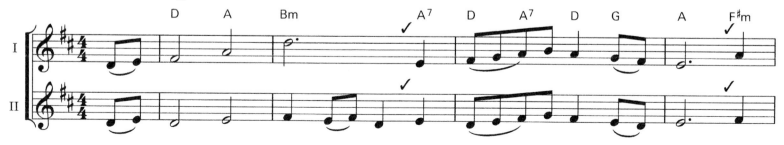

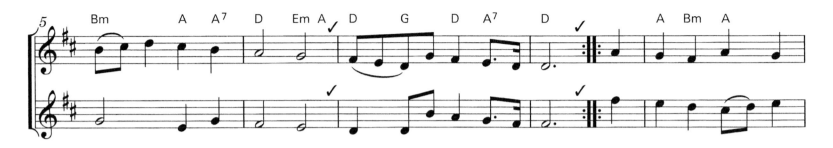
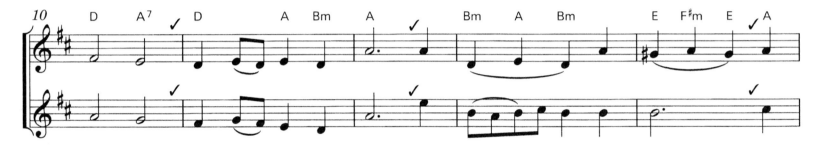
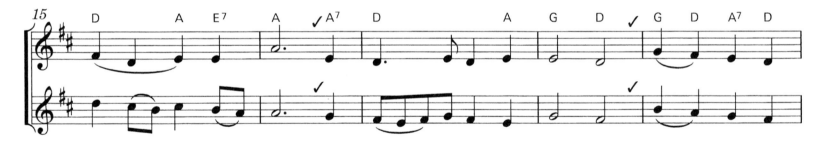
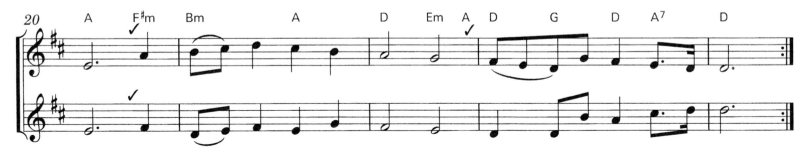

Arima Samba　Pitts

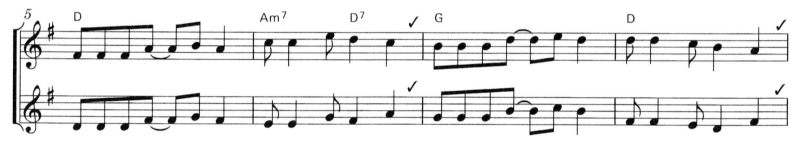

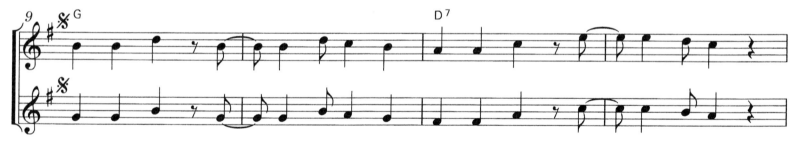

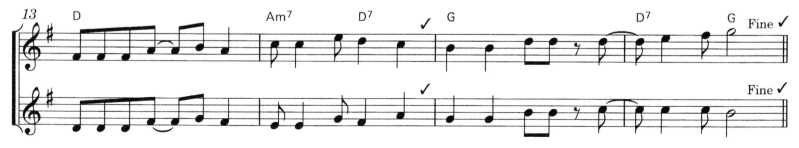

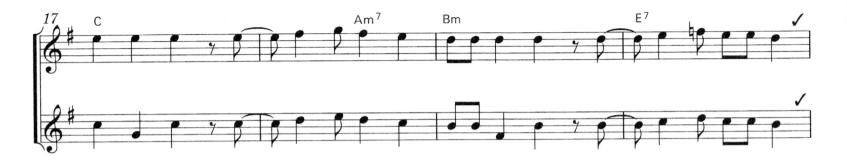

The **samba** is a Brazilian dance with a basic two beats in each bar, strongly syncopated.

The rhythm patterns are usually in two-bar phrases. A special rhythmic feature is the anticipation of the first beat of the second bar of a two-bar pattern, so that this beat comes at the end of the previous bar and is tied over.

Try playing these rhythms, counting carefully. Start by counting in four. Later you should count two slow beats per bar.

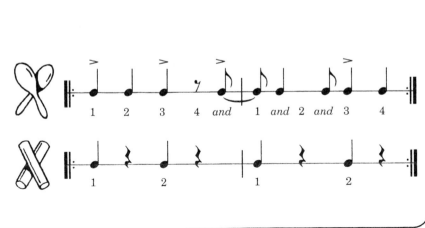

Little Mazurka   *Chopin*

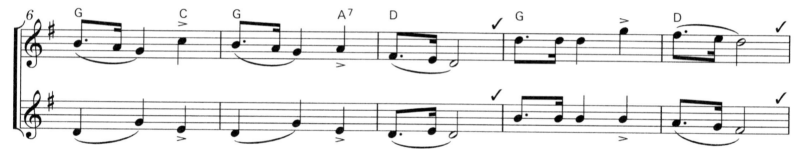

The **mazurka** is a Polish national dance in triple time, often with strong accents falling on the second or third beat, as here. It was adapted for the ballroom in the 18th century. In the 19th century, Chopin was one of the first to popularise it as a piano piece, making use of its characteristic rhythms.

As you play try to emphasise the notes marked with accents. This will help to produce the mazurka rhythm.

2 = Optional alternative fingering. See page 32.

Carman's Whistle   Elizabethan

During the reign of Elizabeth 1st (1558 - 1603) some instrumental music used popular folksongs of the day. 'Carman's Whistle' was used by several composers, including Robert Johnson in his lute music, and by William Byrd in music for virginals (keyboard).

Berceuse   Dvořák

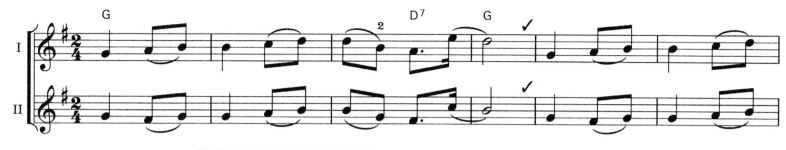

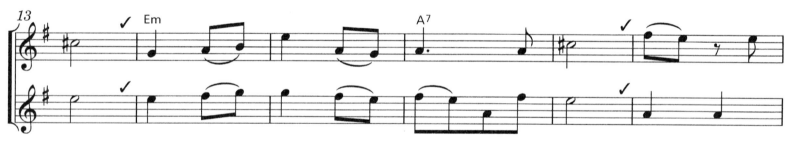

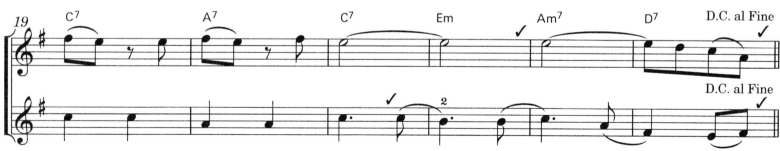

2 = Optional alternative fingering.

Cradle Song   Brahms

Introduction: count 2 bars (see Teacher's Book)

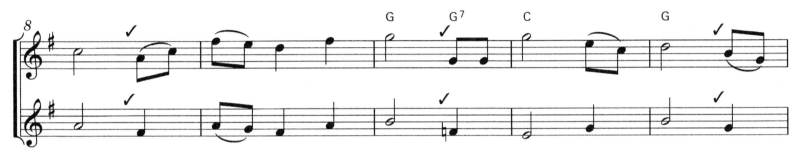

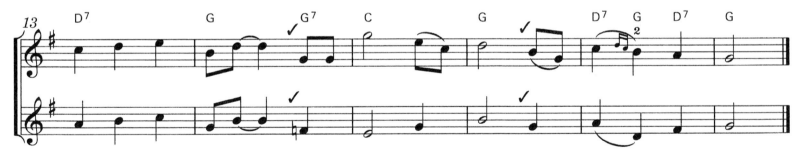

Johannes **Brahms** (1833 - 97) was a German composer. He wrote many songs, including the famous 'Cradle Song', as well as many piano pieces. Brahms also wrote symphonies, concertos and several overtures and small orchestral works. Among the most popular was his 'Variations on a theme of Haydn' (the St Anthony Chorale).

Try to play this piece smoothly, with carefully shaped phrases. Listen to make sure that all your 'pinched notes' are well in tune.

2 = Optional alternative fingering.

Fingering Chart
English (Baroque) Fingered Recorders

Descant (or Tenor)

Finger														2						
Left thumb	●	●	●	●	●	●	●	●	●	●	●	●	●	○	○	○	◐	◐	◐	◐
Left 1st finger	●	●	●	●	●	●	●	●	●	●	●	○	○	●	○	○	●	●	●	●
Left 2nd finger	●	●	●	●	●	●	●	●	●	○	○	●	●	●	●	●	●	●	●	●
Left 3rd finger	●	●	●	●	●	●	●	○	○	●	○	●	○	○	○	●	●	●	●	●
Right 1st finger	●	●	●	●	●	○	○	●	○	●	○	○	○	○	○	●	●	●	○	○
Right 2nd finger	●	●	●	●	○	●	○	●	○	○	○	○	○	○	○	●	●	○	●	○
Right 3rd finger	●	●	⊙	○	●	●	○	○	○	○	○	○	○	○	○	●	○	●	○	○
Right 4th finger	●	○	○	○	●	○	○	○	○	○	○	○	○	○	○	○	○	○	○	○

○ Open hole
● Closed hole
◐ Partly closed hole
2 Alternative fingering